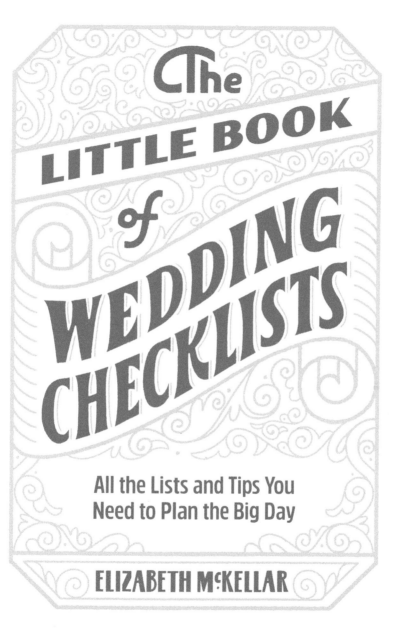

The LITTLE BOOK of WEDDING CHECKLISTS

All the Lists and Tips You
Need to Plan the Big Day

ELIZABETH McKELLAR

ROCKRIDGE
PRESS

Interior and Cover Designer: Julie Schrader
Art Producer: Samantha Ulban
Editor: Emily Angell and Bridget Fitzgerald
Production Editor: Jenna Dutton
Illustrations: © 2020 Mary Kate McDevitt;
Alyssa Nassner, p. 63. Author Photo Courtesy of Wyn Wiley

ISBN: Print 978-1-64611-341-5 | eBook 978-1-64611-342-2
R0

Contents

Introduction

Congratulations on your engagement! Now that the excitement has begun, the next step is to get organized and break down all the parts of planning a wedding into easy, digestible pieces. This planner is meant to provide all the tools that you may need to stay organized, whether you're planning a small ceremony with a larger reception, a city hall visit with a raging dance party, a destination weekend in your favorite place, or a wedding with the whole town at your family home.

The following sections include the essentials and more, which you're free to customize based on your plans. Feel free to cross out anything that doesn't apply to you or to adjust a schedule or task to your own timeline. List not applicable? Skip it! Nowadays everything but the marriage license and officiant are open to interpretation, and you're free to do whatever feels best for you and your partner. At the end of the day, the most important part is that you get to celebrate your way, surrounded by your favorite people.

IDENTIFY YOUR OPTIONS

Here are two lists of wide-ranging elements to consider for your ceremony and reception. Cross out any elements that don't apply and check the ones that do. Asterisks denote the most important pieces to consider.

Ceremony

- ☐ **Essentials***

    - ☐ Marriage license
    - ☐ Officiant
    - ☐ Traditional vows
    - ☐ Self-written vows

- ☐ **Music***

    - ☐ Playlist
    - ☐ Musicians
    - ☐ Special songs

- ☐ **Flower and decor options**

    - ☐ Altar flowers and other decor
    - ☐ Bridal bouquet
    - ☐ Bridal party flowers
    - ☐ Corsages
    - ☐ Boutonnieres

- [ ] Groom boutonnieres
- [ ] Family flowers
- [ ] Miscellaneous flowers
- [ ] Guest book
- [ ] Card box
- [ ] Ceremony program
- [ ] Ceremony signage
- [ ] Seats reserved for immediate family
- [ ] Chair rentals
- [ ] Other decor rentals _____

- [ ] **Ceremony traditions**

  - [ ] Readings
  - [ ] Ceremony rituals
  - [ ] Jumping the broom
  - [ ] Unity candle
  - [ ] Handfasting
  - [ ] Other _____

Reception

- ☐ **Food***

  - ☐ Appetizers
  - ☐ Buffet meal
  - ☐ Family-style meal
  - ☐ Seated/plated meal
  - ☐ Wedding cake
  - ☐ Groom's cake
  - ☐ Alternative desserts
  - ☐ Late-night snacks

- ☐ **Beverages***

  - ☐ Cocktail hour
  - ☐ Beer and wine only
  - ☐ Specialty cocktails
  - ☐ Nonalcoholic drinks
  - ☐ Open bar
  - ☐ Cash bar
  - ☐ Pre-ceremony drinks
  - ☐ Champagne toast

- [ ] **Rentals**
    - [ ] Chairs
    - [ ] Tables
    - [ ] Tablecloths
    - [ ] Table runners
    - [ ] Napkins
    - [ ] Cutlery
    - [ ] Glassware
    - [ ] Lounge seating
    - [ ] Lighting
    - [ ] Dance floor
    - [ ] Tent
    - [ ] Tent liner
    - [ ] Tent walls
    - [ ] Catering tent
    - [ ] Heating and cooling
    - [ ] Extra bathrooms, if needed
- [ ] **Music***
    - [ ] DJ
    - [ ] Band
    - [ ] Playlist

- ☐ **Decor**
  - ☐ Seating chart
  - ☐ Table numbers
  - ☐ Place cards
  - ☐ Menus
  - ☐ Centerpieces
  - ☐ Candles
  - ☐ Bar menus
  - ☐ Dessert signage
  - ☐ Favors

- ☐ **Reception traditions**
  - ☐ Receiving line
  - ☐ Couple introduction
  - ☐ Wedding party introduction
  - ☐ Toast/speeches
  - ☐ First dance
  - ☐ Parents' dances
  - ☐ Bouquet toss
  - ☐ Garter toss
  - ☐ Cake cutting
  - ☐ Grand exit
  - ☐ Other _____

Timelines, whether big or small, are the easiest way to alleviate any worry or stress—and ensure that you're not falling behind schedule. Note that these are guidelines that may seem early or late depending on your location and the type of wedding you're having, so adjust them based on your own schedule. If you're at a total loss about where to start, this is a great way to get on track.

THE BIG TIMELINE

There are a lot of moving parts in wedding planning, but this timeline will help you stay on track. It works as a schedule and shows you where to get started. Each task can be adjusted based on the length of your planning time frame, the popularity of your date, the importance of each item to you, and if you decided to hire a wedding planner.

10 to 12 Months Ahead

☐ Develop a wedding budget

☐ Book a wedding planner

☐ Begin gathering inspiration and ideas

☐ Book your venue

☐ Plan your engagement party (1 to 3 months after your engagement)

7 to 9 Months Ahead

☐ Purchase a wedding dress (if you're wearing a bridal gown)

☐ Finalize and format guest list

☐ Print and mail (or email) save-the-dates

☐ Book photographer

☐ Book DJ/band

☐ Reserve hotel room block

☐ Book hair and makeup vendor

☐ Book caterer and menu tastings

☐ Complete wedding website

4 to 6 Months Ahead

☐ Book florist

☐ Book officiant

☐ Book transportation (buses, getaway vehicle, etc.)

☐ Finalize and purchase bridesmaids' gowns

☐ Purchase any suits or tuxedo attire for the bridal party

☐ Select and order cake

☐ Book ceremony music

- ☐ Book rehearsal dinner venue
- ☐ Complete gift registry
- ☐ Order wedding rings
- ☐ Begin invitation design
- ☐ Brainstorm welcome bags
- ☐ Begin rental design decisions (chairs, linens, place settings, etc.)

2 to 3 Months Ahead

- ☐ Send out invitations (8 to 10 weeks before the wedding is standard)
- ☐ Begin wedding dress alterations (if needed)
- ☐ Finalize ceremony outline and readings
- ☐ Select final design details, including food choices, table assignments, place cards, ceremony programs, signage, favors, out-of-town welcome bags
- ☐ Bridal shower (around 2 months before the wedding generally)
- ☐ Order favors/items for welcome bags

5 to 7 Weeks Ahead

- ☐ Apply for and pick up marriage license (confirm when you can apply with the county clerk's office in the county where you're getting married)
- ☐ Finalize all floral, design, and rental details

- [ ] Design escort cards, ceremony program, and physical menus
- [ ] Bachelor/bachelorette parties (aim for 1 to 4 months pre-wedding)
- [ ] Mail or email rehearsal dinner invitations

4 Weeks Ahead

- [ ] RSVPs due
- [ ] Finalize dinner, bar, and dessert menu design

3 Weeks Ahead

- [ ] Finalize guest count
- [ ] Send updated guest counts to your vendors
- [ ] Create day-of timeline (see pages 12 and 13) and send to vendors
- [ ] Begin seating assignments and edit as final RSVPs arrive
- [ ] Final clothing fittings

2 Weeks Ahead

- [ ] Finalize seating assignments and send escort and place cards to print
- [ ] Begin assembling welcome bags (if needed)
- [ ] Send simplified day-of timeline to bridal party and VIPs
- [ ] Get any haircuts/color needed
- [ ] Pack bags for wedding day, wedding night, and honeymoon

1 Week Ahead

☐ Relax! Ideally, you'll be prepped and ready with this week to relax and tend to any last-minute items. Building in some buffer time will allow for the unexpected to pop up, and you will still have enough space and time to enjoy the days leading up to your wedding.

Wedding Week

☐ Get married!

THE DAY-OF TIMELINE

Equally important and more detailed than the big timeline, the day-of timeline is a typical rundown of the wedding day, from getting dressed all the way to your grand exit. This can become the schedule you give to vendors, and you can create a simplified version for the wedding party, family, or VIPs. Fill in the schedule as it applies to your plans by starting with the scheduled times (such as when the ceremony begins or when the vendors are scheduled) and working backward.

Day Before

_____ Rehearsal start time
_____ Rehearsal dinner start time

Day Of

_____ Setup of event begins
_____ Hair and makeup begins
_____ Hair and makeup ends

_____ Bride steps into dress

_____ Rentals arrive

_____ Florals arrive

_____ Caterer arrives

_____ Bridal party is dressed

_____ Photographer arrives

_____ DJ/band arrives

_____ Bridal party arrives at venue

_____ First look (if applicable)

_____ Bride and groom portraits

_____ Bridal party portraits

_____ Guests begin to arrive

_____ Ceremony begins

_____ Cocktail hour/family photos

_____ Guests invited to dinner (ideal timing for outdoor weddings coincides with sunset)

_____ Dinner served

_____ Toasts

_____ First dance

_____ Parents' dances

_____ Open dancing

_____ Cake cutting

_____ Photography ends

_____ Final song

_____ Bride and groom exit

_____ Vendor strike

TIP: Every time you need people to move from one location to another—for example, from the ceremony to cocktail hour in a different location—build an extra 20 minutes into your timeline.

BUDGET

The budget is the puzzle piece that will affect every part of your wedding planning adventure and is best addressed before hiring any vendors, or making any commitments. Think of this as an opportunity to decide where you want to invest your money, which pieces truly matter, and allow these priorities to guide your decision making. By beginning with this step, you'll get one of the trickier pieces out of the way and ultimately have a clear game plan to move forward!

BUDGET PLANNING

Looking at the big picture is the first step to approaching your wedding budget. These questions will help you and your partner get on the same page about the total budget and the decision-making process.

☐   What is your overall budget number? _____

☐   Is this budget number fixed or flexible? _____

☐ What does that budget include or not include? (Honeymoon, dress, attire, etc.)

_____

_____

☐ Who has final financial decision-making power? (Who is Chief Financial Officer of the wedding?)

_____

☐ Do you make budget decisions along the way, or are you only selecting vendors that fit into this number?

_____

☐ Are there other sources, favors, or negotiations that can contribute to the final number?

_____

_____

BUDGET HACK: Picking an off date, an off-season, or even an early weekday for your wedding will save you a chunk in every category and will have vendors far more likely to negotiate their costs. It never hurts to ask!

WHERE IS OUR MONEY GOING?

This comprehensive list of budget categories and percentage break-downs is a starting point; cross out anything you're skipping and redistribute the percentage to the items that matter most to you.

Planning (5%)

	ESTIMATE	FINAL
☐ Wedding planner or coordinator		

Venue and Catering (50%)

	ESTIMATE	FINAL
☐ Ceremony venue		
☐ Reception venue		
☐ Rentals (chairs, tables, linens, tabletop, etc.)		
☐ Catering		
☐ Alcohol		
☐ Cake/dessert		

Documentation (12%)

	ESTIMATE	FINAL
☐ Photography		
☐ Videography		

Reception Entertainment (7%)

	ESTIMATE	FINAL
☐ Reception music (band, DJ, other)		

Transportation (2%)

ESTIMATE	FINAL

☐ Transportation (shuttles, getaway car, etc.)

Ceremony (2%)

ESTIMATE	FINAL

☐ Officiant

☐ Music

Attire and Beauty (8%)

ESTIMATE	FINAL

☐ Dress

☐ Tuxedo or suit

☐ Hair and makeup

Floral and Decor (8%)

ESTIMATE	FINAL

☐ Flowers

☐ Day-of decor (programs, signage, ribbons, escort cards, etc.)

☐ Lighting

SECRET SPEND: Delivery charges are a surprise that often arrives closer to the wedding, so remember to get an accurate quote for rentals or vendor pickups for the appropriate end time of your event. Late nights and weekends often have an extra charge, while pickups from Monday to Friday are much cheaper if your venue allows it.

Bonus Round: Gratuities (6%)

These are suggestions, but gratuities are entirely at your discretion.

	ESTIMATE	FINAL
☐ Photographer: $50 to $100 per photographer		
☐ Videographer: $50 to $100 per videographer		
☐ Catering: 15% to 20% of overall food cost only (not service). This is sometimes included in the contract.		
☐ Cake: 10% to 15% of cost (optional)		
☐ Ceremony music: $25 per musician		
☐ DJ/band: $50 per musician		
☐ Officiant: $50 to $100 or gift		
☐ Transportation: Often included in contract		
☐ Hair and makeup: 15% to 20% of cost		
☐ Lighting: $25 per person setting up and breaking down		
☐ Rental deliveries: $25 per delivery person		

GUEST LIST

The guest list is an obvious way to keep the budget in check, but
that may not be possible for those with a large family, a hometown
wedding, or parents having the final say over the guest list. Here is a
quick list to get you started—and keep in mind that whoever is footing
the wedding bill often has final say over extra invitations.

Tier 1

☐ Immediate family

    ☐ Parents

    ☐ Stepparents

    ☐ Siblings

☐ Close friends

Tier 2

☐ Extended family

    ☐ Aunts

    ☐ Uncles

    ☐ Cousins and Second Cousins

☐ Work friends

☐ College friends

☐ Parents' friends

☐ Family friends

Additional Questions

Close work friends versus the whole office?

_____

Are children and plus-ones invited?

_____

Note: *For plus-ones, the general rule of thumb is that if the invited guest is married, engaged, or cohabitating, they receive a plus-one. If a guest has been with their partner for less than a year, it's appropriate to invite just the guest. Oftentimes this is a tricky subject—use your discretion or choose a hard line, but do whatever feels right.*

> **TIP:** The guest list is often a hot topic, and it's best to be as gently ruthless as possible. If you plan on sending invitations to "B-list" guests, you run the risk of them finding out that they're not a top pick. Invite them to another event and keep the invitation list to A-list guests only.

INVITATIONS

Invitations can be a fun way to set the tone for your wedding. There are endless options for invitations—whether physical or digital—but the most important things to ensure are that they contain all the information your guests need and that they receive them in a timely manner. These samples will give you a good starting point.

Invitations Two Ways

☐ Informal

TOGETHER
WITH THEIR FAMILIES

Invitee names (parents, if applicable)

JOHN DOE
— AND —
JANE SMITH

Couple's names

INVITE YOU TO SHARE IN THEIR JOY
AS THEY ARE UNITED IN MARRIAGE

Date

Time

SATURDAY, OCTOBER 9, 2021
at 6:30 P.M.

Location of ceremony and reception

CENTRAL COUNTRY CLUB
RECEPTION TO FOLLOW

RSVP information
(separate RSVP card,
email address, or
website contact)

RSVP:
johnandjanewedding@gmail.com

The wedding website and
additional wedding details
can be communicated on a
separate card, or on the back
of an informal invitation.

Invitee names (parents, if applicable)

Couple's names

MR. AND MRS. SMITH INVITE YOU TO SHARE IN THEIR JOY AT THE MARRIAGE OF THEIR DAUGHTER

Jane Marie

TO

Johnathan Matthew Doe

Date / Time

Saturday, October 9, 2021

AT 6:30 P.M.

Location of ceremony and reception

Central Country Club

1300 COUNTRY LANE

EVERYTOWN, PA 12300

For formal invitations, include a separate card that lists a wedding website for details including attire/ dress code, gift registry, hotel information, transportation, activities (for destination weddings), maps and directions

DINNER AND DANCING

TO FOLLOW

For formal invitations, include a separate RSVP card. You can also use a separate card for an informal invitation, or you can provide an email address or website contact.

Kindly Reply

PLEASE RESPOND BY THE 30TH OF JULY

NAME(S)_____

_____ WILL ATTEND

_____ REGRETFULLY DECLINES

Invitation Timelines

- [ ] **Destination wedding**

  - [ ] Save-the-date: 8 to 12 months prior to wedding
  - [ ] Invitation: 10 to 12 weeks prior

- [ ] **Standard wedding**

  - [ ] Save-the-date: 8 to 10 months prior to wedding
  - [ ] Invitation: 8 to 10 weeks prior

- [ ] **Hometown wedding**

  - [ ] Save-the-date: 4 to 6 months prior to wedding
  - [ ] Invitation: 6 to 8 weeks prior

One of the first and most important decisions, your venue sets the tone for both your wedding and your to-do list for your planning journey. While your venue may or may not be the same for your ceremony and reception, there are practical considerations such as inclusions (rentals, etc.) or vendor requirements that are important to keep in mind while comparing your options. These questions are intended to suss out some of the surprises you may not think about, ensuring you can make the most informed and empowered decision.

CEREMONY QUESTIONS

Here's a list of questions to ask when visiting each potential ceremony location. Asking the same questions makes it easier to compare.

Is my preferred date available? _____

What is the rental fee? _____

What is the seated capacity of the space (comfortable guest count versus maximum capacity)?

_____

Is there on-site parking? _____

Are there any considerations or notes about accessibility for guests with restricted mobility?

_____

Do you provide a ceremony coordinator? _____

Are any rentals included (chairs, in-house sound systems, etc.)?

_____

When can we arrive and how late can we stay?

_____

If outdoors, do you provide electricity? _____

How many bathrooms are there? _____

Can we bring in a DJ or musicians?

_____

Can we hold a rehearsal? When do these usually take place?

_____

Is there an additional fee to use the space for a rehearsal?

_____

Are there any other events going on the same day?

_____

If outdoors, where does the sun set and what is the lighting like during the ceremony?

Are there any restrictions or limitations that we should know about (decorations, noise, etc.)?

Do you have any required or limited vendors that we need to work with?

What is the cancellation policy?

RECEPTION QUESTIONS

Take this list of questions along when you visit potential reception locations. Asking the same questions makes it easier to compare.

Is my preferred date available? _____

What is the rental fee? _____

How much is the deposit? _____

How many hours are included with the site rental? When can we arrive and how late can we stay?

_____

Do you have an on-site coordinator? If yes, what is their role?

_____

Are any rentals included (tables, chairs, plates, and flatware)?

_____

_____

Are there any hidden fees (service charges, cleaning fees, gratuities, and taxes)?

_____

_____

What is the rain plan?

_____

TIP: While sticker shock for an all-inclusive venue is real, oftentimes when every DIY element is calculated, the piecemeal approach can cost more.

What is the seated capacity of the space (comfortable guest count versus maximum capacity)?

_____

Is there a space for cocktail hour, and is it included in the rental?

_____

Are any other events happening on our date?

_____

Is there required on-site catering or can we bring in our own?

_____

Is there a food and beverage minimum? _____

Can we purchase our own alcohol for the bar? _____

Are there any noise restrictions? _____

Are there any decor restrictions (candles, etc.)?

_____

_____

Is there a required vendor list?

_____

Can I bring a cake or desserts from an outside source? _____

How many bathrooms are there? _____

Is there on-site parking? _____

Do you have liability insurance? _____

What is the cancellation policy?

_____

SECRET SPEND: Always ask about service charges, gratuities, and food and beverage minimums, as these hidden fees can add up significantly and it's best to plan for them in advance.

COMPARE VENUES

Fill in these lists for each venue. Seeing everything in one place could help make a tough decision easier.

VENUE NAME

_____

VENUE ADDRESS _____

PRIMARY CONTACT (phone and email)

_____

DATES AVAILABLE _____

EVENT (ceremony, reception, or ceremony and reception)

_____

COST_____

DEPOSIT_____

EXTRA FEES (service charge, etc.)

_____

CAPACITY_____

STAFF PROVIDED (day-of coordinator, waitstaff, bartenders)

_____

PARKING_____

ON-SITE CATERING _____

EXCLUSIVE USE OR SHARED _____

NOTES

_____

_____

_____

VENUE NAME

_____

VENUE ADDRESS _____

PRIMARY CONTACT (phone and email)

_____

DATES AVAILABLE _____

EVENT (ceremony, reception, or ceremony and reception)

_____

COST_____

DEPOSIT_____

EXTRA FEES (service charge, etc.)

_____

CAPACITY _____

STAFF PROVIDED (day-of coordinator, waitstaff, bartenders)

_____

PARKING _____

ON-SITE CATERING _____

EXCLUSIVE USE OR SHARED _____

NOTES

_____

_____

_____

VENUE NAME

_____

VENUE ADDRESS _____

PRIMARY CONTACT (phone and email)

_____

DATES AVAILABLE _____

EVENT (ceremony, reception, or ceremony and reception)

_____

COST_____

DEPOSIT_____

EXTRA FEES (service charge, etc.)

_____

CAPACITY_____

STAFF PROVIDED (day-of coordinator, waitstaff, bartenders)

_____

PARKING_____

ON-SITE CATERING _____

EXCLUSIVE USE OR SHARED _____

NOTES

_____

_____

_____

_____

_____

_____

Vendors are the backbone of your wedding. It's important to invest in an experienced vendor team that will allow you to enjoy your wedding day knowing that everything is handled! If your venue doesn't have an in-house coordinator—and you're not working with a planner—it's crucial to remember that you'll end up being the point person for each vendor. Finally, here is one note on friends or family as vendors: They may be excited and willing to help, but having a contract and agreeing to some form of compensation is the best way to ensure that everything goes smoothly.

THE OFFICIANT

Choosing the person to marry you and your partner is a choice for both the head and heart. These lists will help you choose an officiant by asking important questions, making sure they're licensed, and communicating to ensure that you and your partner have the ceremony you both envisioned.

Questions for Your Officiant

Are you legally able to perform a wedding in our state?

_____

Do you have a script or do you personalize each ceremony?

_____

How do you create the ceremony, and how much input
do we have?

_____

Can we write our own vows? _____

How long is your typical ceremony?

_____

Do you come to the rehearsal?

_____

What do you wear for the ceremony?

_____

What time do you arrive on the wedding day?

_____

Will you fill out and file our marriage license?

_____

What is your backup plan if you are sick or have emergency circumstances?

_____

What are your fees/deposits?

_____

How to Prepare for a Friend Officiant

- ☐ Is it legal to have my friend officiate in my wedding state/location? (Call up the county clerk's office in the county where you'll be getting married or check their website to confirm.)

- ☐ Confirm that your friend is officially ordained via their online certification source (they should get a certificate)

- ☐ Register your friend with the court, if necessary

- ☐ Work with your friend on writing the ceremony

- ☐ Discuss what your friend should wear

- ☐ If it's your friend's first wedding, practice with them before the rehearsal

- ☐ Make sure your friend signs and returns the marriage license per your state's requirements

Friend Officiant Checklist

- ☐ Get ordained

- ☐ Call the county clerk

- ☐ Create a timeline

- [ ] Discuss the couples' vision for their ceremony
- [ ] Write the ceremony (it should be about 15 to 20 minutes long)
- [ ] Finalize the ceremony with the couple
- [ ] Rehearse
- [ ] Perform the ceremony
- [ ] Sign and return the marriage license

FOOD AND DRINK

There are many options and factors to consider when selecting a vendor that you trust to handle what your guests will eat and drink at your reception. These questions will help you stay organized when you meet with potential caterers. Plus, asking the same questions makes it easier to compare.

Questions for the Caterer

Have you ever worked at our wedding venue?

If you have, are there any surprises or notes that you feel we should be aware of?

What is the price range for stations and buffet, family-style, and plated meals?

Do you work mainly off of pre-designed menus, or can you create a menu based on style or dietary requirements?

_____

How many appetizers do you recommend per person during cocktail hour?

_____

What's the cost difference for passed appetizers versus stations?

_____

How much food do you allot or recommend per person based on the style of food service (buffet, plated dinner, stations, family-style meal, etc.)?

_____

Do the quoted prices include service, labor, and any necessary rentals (including any kitchen or service rentals)?

_____

How and when is the food prepared? Is it prepared off-site and transported, or is there any preparation or finishing on-site?

_____

When do you need the final guest count? _____

Do you provide bartending services? If so, are these additional or included in any of the price ranges previously quoted?

_____

> **BUDGET HACK:** If your venue allows for it, buyng your own alcohol is the best way to save some money, and you can return any unopened or unchilled bottles afterwards. Once beer, white wine, or sparkling wine has been chilled it oftentimes cannot be returned. However, check your local liquor stores' policies to confirm.

For bartending and alcohol options, do you offer per-person packages only, or is there an option to purchase the alcohol ourselves, while you provide staff, mixers, ice, etc.?

_____

What are the different price ranges for a full bar versus beer and wine or a cash bar?

_____

If doing a buffet, how many buffet setups do you recommend?

_____

How early does your staff arrive on the wedding day?

_____

How much do vendor meals cost?

_____

Are gratuities, taxes, and service fees included?

_____

Do you have up-to-date liability insurance? _____

What do you require to reserve a date, and what is the deposit and payment schedule?

_____

_____

TIP: Make sure your caterer quotes you the full amount, including fees, taxes, and gratuities. Add an extra 10% into the catering budget for any unforeseen circumstances or last-minute changes.

BAR COMPARISON

Full Bar	Partial Bar	Cash Bar
Biggest range for guests' tastes	You can choose a signature drink, plus wine and beer	Guests purchase their own drinks
You don't have to include every major alcohol option; include those that your guests will drink	A signature drink shows off your personality and theme of the wedding	Though common in certain areas or cultures, some guests may be unfamiliar with this
Most expensive option	Cost of the bar is controlled, guests still have options such as specialty cocktails at cocktail hour only.	Most cost-effective option

FOOD AND DRINK VENDOR COMPARISON

Complete this chart to compare caterers. Seeing everything side by side could help make a tough decision easier.

Guest Count: _____

VENDOR

Company name _____

Contact name _____

Address _____

Phone number _____

Email _____

Have they worked at venue before? _____

☐ Food

_____ Price per person: Plated meal
_____ Price per person: Buffet meal

☐ **Bar**

Cost per person for the following:

_____ Open bar

_____ Cash bar

_____ Beer/wine

_____ BYOB

_____ Other

_____ Bar service or setup cost

☐ **Fees**

_____ Gratuities

_____ Service charges

_____ Deposit amount

_____ Any other fees?

☐ **Rental**

_____ Kitchen and serving needs

_____ What rentals does this include? Do you provide tabletop rentals (plates, flatware, glassware, etc.), and is this included in the provided price ranges? Are all rentals required to go through your company?

☐ **Service**

_____ Number of waitstaff

_____ Number of bartenders? Do you provide bartending services? If so, are these additional or included in any of the price ranges previously quoted?

_____ Cleanup? Yes/No

_____ Additional service/cleanup fees

VENDOR

Company name _____

Contact name _____

Address _____

Phone number _____

Email _____

Have they worked at venue before? _____

☐ **Food**

_____ Price per person: Plated meal
_____ Price per person: Buffet meal

☐ **Bar**

Cost per person for the following:
_____ Open bar
_____ Cash bar
_____ Beer/wine
_____ BYOB
_____ Other
_____ Bar service or setup cost

☐ **Fees**

_____ Gratuities
_____ Service charges
_____ Deposit amount
_____ Any other fees?

☐ Rental

_____ Kitchen and serving needs
_____ What rentals does this include? Do you provide tabletop rentals (plates, flatware, glassware, etc.), and is this included in the provided price ranges? Are all rentals required to go through your company?

☐ Service

_____ Number of waitstaff
_____ Number of bartenders? Do you provide bartending services? If so, are these additional or included in any of the price ranges previously quoted?
_____ Cleanup? Yes/No
_____ Additional service/cleanup fees

VENDOR

Company name _____

Contact name _____

Address _____

Phone number _____

Email _____

Have they worked at venue before? _____

☐ **Food**

_____ Price per person: Plated meal
_____ Price per person: Buffet meal

☐ **Bar**

Cost per person for the following:
_____ Open bar
_____ Cash bar
_____ Beer/wine
_____ BYOB
_____ Other
_____ Bar service or setup cost

☐ **Fees**

_____ Gratuities
_____ Service charges
_____ Deposit amount
_____ Any other fees?

☐ **Rental**

_____ Kitchen and serving needs
_____ What rentals does this include? Do you
provide tabletop rentals (plates, flatware,
glassware, etc.), and is this included in the
provided price ranges? Are all rentals required
to go through your company?

☐ **Service**

_____ Number of waitstaff
_____ Number of bartenders? Do you provide bartending services? If so, are these additional or included in any of the price ranges previously quoted?
_____ Cleanup? Yes/No
_____ Additional service/cleanup fees

VENDOR

Company name _____

Contact name _____

Address _____

Phone number _____

Email _____

Have they worked at venue before? _____

☐ **Food**

_____ Price per person: Plated meal
_____ Price per person: Buffet meal

☐ **Bar**

Cost per person for the following:
_____ Open bar
_____ Cash bar
_____ Beer/wine

_____ BYOB
_____ Other
_____ Bar service or setup cost

☐ **Fees**

_____ Gratuities
_____ Service charges
_____ Deposit amount
_____ Any other fees?

☐ **Rental**

_____ Kitchen and serving needs
_____ What rentals does this include? Do you
provide tabletop rentals (plates, flatware,
glassware, etc.), and is this included in the
provided price ranges? Are all rentals required
to go through your company?

☐ **Service**

_____ Number of waitstaff
_____ Number of bartenders? Do you provide
bartending services? If so, are these
additional or included in any of the price
ranges previously quoted?
_____ Cleanup? Yes/No
_____ Additional service/cleanup fees

SECRET SPEND: Be sure to check your vendors'
contracts to confirm if they require meals and let your
caterer know. Happy vendors are well-fed vendors.

MUSIC

Music sets the tone for your wedding—from the ceremony to the cocktail hour and reception—and deciding between live music, a DJ, or a playlist depends on a number of factors. Here's a comparison that describes the pros and cons of each.

MUSIC COMPARISON

Live Music	DJ	Playlist
Most expensive option; often has a set range of songs (Top 40, etc.)	Less expensive than a band	Most cost-effective
Brings a lot of energy and experience to the wedding	Great for those who love dancing	Great for picking your favorite music
Specialty songs may take time and cost extra	Biggest variety of music	Advisable to have a troubleshooting plan if anything goes wrong
Can play ceremony music for an extra fee	Will often also play your ceremony for a nominal fee	Someone from the wedding would need to supervise at all times

QUESTIONS FOR THE LIVE MUSICIANS

If you've opted for live musicians, here are some questions to ask the main band contact to see if they're the right fit.

What is your deposit/cancellation policy?

_____

How many hours are included in your price? _____

What is the cost for additional hours? _____

Have you played at the venue before? _____

Do you act as the emcee? _____

How would you motivate a crowd at a reception that is not dancing?

_____

Do you require a stage, and how big of a space do you need to perform?

_____

How do you handle technical elements that go wrong?

_____

Do you bring backup equipment? _____

How involved can we be in the music selection?

_____

What is your music-selection process?

_____

Can we create a "do not play" list? _____

Do you take requests on the day? _____

How early do you arrive to set up? _____

Are you insured? _____

How and where would you like your vendor meals?

_____

What is your wardrobe for our wedding?

_____

Do you have a wireless microphone we can use for toasts?

_____

Do you bring any additional decor or lighting for the
dance party?

_____

Are there any other specifics I should know about?

_____

_____

_____

_____

QUESTIONS FOR THE DJ

If you've decided to go with a DJ, here is a list of questions you should ask to help decide if the vendor can meet your needs.

Will you or an associate be the DJ at our wedding?

_____

What is your deposit/cancellation policy?

_____

How many hours are included in your price? _____

What is the cost for additional hours?

_____

Have you played at the venue before? _____

Do you act as the emcee? _____

How would you motivate a crowd that is not dancing?

_____

Do you have an assistant or backup person if something goes wrong?

_____

Do you bring backup equipment? _____

How involved can we be in the music selection?

_____

What is your music-selection process?

_____

Can we create a "do not play" list? _____

Do you take requests on the day? _____

How early do you arrive to set up? _____

Are you insured? _____

How and where would you like your vendor meals?

_____

What is your wardrobe for our wedding?

_____

Do you have a wireless microphone we can use for toasts?

_____

Do you bring any additional decor or lighting for the
dance party?

_____

Are there any other specifics I should know about?

_____

PHOTO AND VIDEO

If you want someone to capture and record your wedding day, you'll need a photographer and possibly a videographer. Here are questions to help you decide which services you'll want, and to help you find the right photographer and/or videographer to document the day.

Questions for the Photographer

Will you or an associate be photographing our wedding?

_____

How many other weddings will you
photograph that weekend? _____

Do you have an assistant or second photographer?

_____

What is your cancellation policy?

_____

What does your photo retouching consist of?

_____

How long after the wedding will I receive the images?

_____

Who owns the rights to the images? _____

Have you ever worked at the venue? _____

Have you worked with any of my other vendors before?

_____

Do you include an engagement session? If not,
how much would that cost?

_____

How many hours are included, and what is the cost for
extra hours?

_____

What is your deposit? _____

Do you carry backup equipment? _____

Can we request a shot list? _____

Will you be posting our photos on social media
or submitting them to blogs and publications?

_____

_____

Questions for the Videographer

Will you or an associate videographer
be documenting our wedding? _____

_____

How many other weddings will you document that weekend?

_____

Do you have an assistant or second videographer?

_____

What is your cancellation policy?

_____

How long after the wedding will I receive the footage?

_____

Who owns the rights to the footage? _____

Have you ever filmed at the venue? _____

Have you worked with any of my other vendors before?

_____

How many hours are included, and what is the cost for
extra hours?

_____

What is your deposit? _____

Do you carry backup equipment? _____

Can we request a shot list? _____

Will you be posting our videos on social media or submitting
them to blogs and publications?

_____

_____

CRITERIA FOR VIDEO

If you check off any of the following as must-haves in your mind, then video might be something you want to work into your budget:

☐ Live record of ceremony and vows

☐ Live record of toasts

☐ Live record of dances

☐ Getting the overall vibe of ceremony and reception, especially dancing

FLOWERS AND DECOR

Do you *need* flowers or additional decor? Not necessarily—you do you! However, if you do want them, here's a list to go through to determine which pieces work best for you.

Flowers

☐ **Personal flowers**

☐ Bridal bouquet(s)

☐ Bridesmaids' bouquets (#: _____)

☐ Groom boutonniere(s)

☐ Boutonnieres, corsages, or bouquets for the groomsmen, parents, ushers, or officiant (#: _____/#: _____/#: _____)

☐ Flower girl petals or mini bouquet

- ☐ **Decorative flowers**

  - ☐ Ceremony altar
  - ☐ Pew or chair arrangements (#: _____)
  - ☐ Aisle flowers (#: _____)

- ☐ **Reception flowers**

  - ☐ Cocktail tables (#: _____)
  - ☐ Centerpieces for reception (#: _____)
  - ☐ Head table
  - ☐ Cake/dessert table
  - ☐ Guest book table
  - ☐ Seating assignment table
  - ☐ Bar decor

Decor

- ☐ **Lighting**

  - ☐ Candles (if venue allows, or LED candles)
  - ☐ String lights
  - ☐ Uplights
  - ☐ Gobo (custom monogram on the dance floor or wall)
  - ☐ Lanterns
  - ☐ Chandeliers

- ☐ Favors
- ☐ Drapery
- ☐ Paper goods

  - ☐ Ceremony program
  - ☐ Menu
  - ☐ Place cards/escort cards
  - ☐ Signage

These days, "wedding attire" is an open book of possibilities—anything goes, and you have a lot of creative freedom. From location and season, to style and formality level, there are many opportunities to play up your own personality and style in ways that feel right for you. That being said, this section will address much of that flexibility, as well as the traditional bridal elements and references to answer any questions you may have.

YOU AND YOUR PARTNER

Here is a list to begin thinking about the pieces of your wedding attire. The only rule these days is that you feel like yourself and love what you're wearing.

Partner #1

If wearing a gown:

☐ Gown _____

☐ Shoes _____

☐ Veil _____

- ☐ Garter
- ☐ Headpiece (headband or hair clips)

_____

- ☐ Bra/shapewear _____
- ☐ Jewelry (earrings, necklace, bracelet)

_____

- ☐ Makeup/hair needs: _____

If wearing a tux/suit/other:

- ☐ Tux/suit/separates _____
- ☐ Shoes _____
- ☐ Bow tie/necktie/other: _____
- ☐ Cuff links
- ☐ Pocket square
- ☐ Other _____
- ☐ Jewelry (earrings, necklace, bracelet)

_____

- ☐ Makeup/hair needs: _____

Partner #2

If wearing a gown:

☐ Gown _____

☐ Shoes _____

☐ Veil _____

☐ Garter

☐ Headpiece (headband or hair clips)

_____

☐ Bra/shapewear _____

☐ Jewelry (earrings, necklace, bracelet)

_____

☐ Makeup/hair needs: _____

_____

If wearing a tux/suit/other:

☐ Tux/suit/separates

_____

☐ Shoes _____

☐ Bow tie/necktie/other: _____

☐ Cuff links

☐ Pocket square

☐ Other _____

☐ Jewelry (earrings, necklace, bracelet)

_____

☐ Makeup/hair needs:

_____

> **TIP:** Choose attire that flatters your silhouette and style and makes sense for your wedding venue. Season, temperature, and formality all play into what kind of attire makes sense for both of you and your guests.

WEDDING DRESS CHEAT SHEET

There are a lot of terms that you encounter when you start dress shopping. Here are some definitions and recommendations for each.

1. **A-Line:** Perfect for all figures and complements those with a larger bust. Classic silhouette.

2. **Ball Gown:** Fitted bodice and dramatic full skirt. Emphasizes the waistline and helps create the hourglass figure. Not recommended for those on the shorter side.

3. **Empire:** Cuts right below the bust. Suited for brides with a smaller bust and for brides wanting less definition and more flow around their stomach and hips.

4. **Mermaid:** Contours the body from the chest to the knee. Perfect for brides who want to accentuate their curves. While sexy, mermaid dresses can be difficult to move in.

5. **Sheath:** Best worn by lean figures, both short and tall. Not very forgiving if you are trying to hide something and doesn't offer any support. Light, easy to move in, and elongates the figure.

6. **Trumpet:** Flares below the hips, creating a partially full skirt. Great for those who want the fit of a mermaid but the flare of a ball gown. Looser around the hips and knees and is easier to move in than a mermaid.

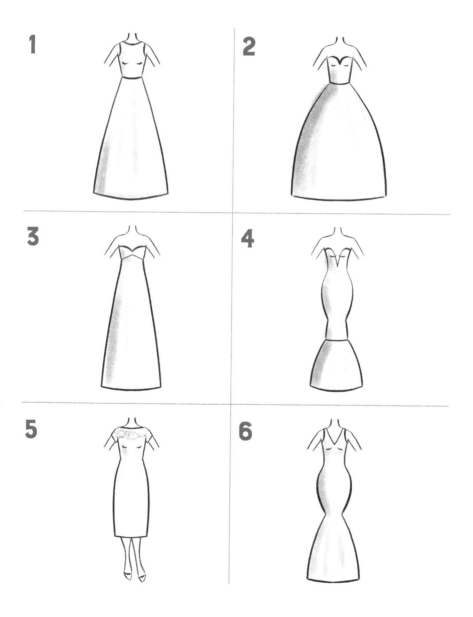

QUESTIONS FOR THE BRIDAL SALON

Are visits by appointment only?

_____

How long do the appointments last? _____

Do you charge for appointments? _____

Do you have a limit to the number of guests I can bring?
(One to two people are best; more may overwhelm you)

_____

What is the price range of your gowns?

_____

Is there a specific aesthetic that you specialize in (e.g., timeless
and classic, indie and unique, relaxed/bohemian, sexy and
sophisticated, etc.)?

_____

Do you have shoes and bras to try on
with the gowns, or should I bring my own? _____

QUESTIONS FOR THE TAILOR/SEAMSTRESS

How far in advance of my wedding should
I book my appointment? _____

How many fittings should I expect? (differs with gown style and needs)

_____

FITTING SCHEDULE

If you purchase your dress from a store or online, you'll ideally have 3 or 4 fittings. For longer engagements, start 4 months before your wedding. For shorter engagements, keep the same number of fittings but condense the timeframe. Your final fitting should be 2 weeks prior to your wedding.

Fitting 1: _____

Fitting 2: _____

Fitting 3: _____

Fitting 4: _____

STORY HOUR: A bride friend purchased a custom dress from a designer that had dressed a number of celebrity brides, but she never looked at reviews or checked the Better Business Bureau for previous issues. Her final dress looked nothing like other finished dresses, but disaster was averted after a visit to a local bridal salon snagged her a perfect sample dress in her size! The moral of this story is to do your due diligence and check references for custom work and customer service to give you peace of mind.

WEDDING PARTY

From matching dresses to anything they choose, dressing the wedding party today is an open field of options. Here are some ideas to get you started.

- ☐ Traditional and formal weddings typically have all matching bridesmaids in the same style dress, with groomsmen wearing neckties or bow ties that match the bridesmaids.

- ☐ Modern weddings are allowing for more freedom with wardrobe. Give your bridesmaids a color palette and a brand of dress to choose from and watch them create a unique set of wardrobe choices that looks good on everyone.

- ☐ Style your bridesmaids to complement your venue and decor. The wedding party is a great way to add color and fun to your celebration.

- ☐ For men's styling, feel free to accessorize. Men are opting for hats, suspenders, and any kind of color and pattern combination—have fun with this!

- ☐ Above all, you want everyone to be happy, comfortable, and confident—this is an area that is really up to you, and there aren't many hard and fast rules.

GUEST CODE

Dress codes for weddings are confusing. Here is a list of the different options to pick from and give your guests if they have any questions.

1. **White tie:** Most formal dress code. Men should wear a tailcoat, formal white shirt, white vest, and white bow tie, along with black formal shoes and white gloves for dancing. Women should wear a formal floor-length ball gown.

2. **Black tie:** Most common formal dress code and indicates an evening wedding. Men should wear a tuxedo with a cummerbund and a black bow tie, and patent leather shoes are also suggested. Women can wear a formal cocktail dress or a floor-length evening gown.

3. **Formal/black tie optional:** Suggests a wedding that is less formal than black tie. A tuxedo, although not required, is still appropriate, or else men can wear a dark suit and tie with a white shirt. Women are free to wear a long dress, formal separates, a dressy suit, or a cocktail-length dress.

4. **Semiformal/cocktail:** If attire isn't specified on the invitation, this is often the default dress code. Depending on the time of the wedding, this is between formal and casual. If the wedding is between 4 p.m. and 5 p.m., wearing something that transitions from day to night is a good bet. A dark suit and tie for men and a cocktail dress or long skirt and top for women are all appropriate.

5. **Casual:** Oftentimes this means anything goes, but staying away from jeans, tank tops, and shorts is implied unless specifically requested. Men can aim for dress pants and a button-down or polo shirt, and women can wear a sundress or a skirt or pants with a nice blouse.

THE DAY-OF BAG

Pre-planning and packing the following items will ease your mind, allowing you to be prepared for any surprise that may pop up. Feel free to hand off both of these lists to a trusted bridal party member or family member.

- ☐ Rings
- ☐ Vows
- ☐ Extra shoes
- ☐ Marriage license, pen, and envelope with prepaid postage to mail everything
- ☐ Tips for vendors (put in individually labeled envelopes for easy distribution)
- ☐ Extra copies of day-of timeline

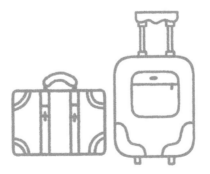

THE EMERGENCY KIT

- ☐ Pain reliever, such as ibuprofen (Advil)
- ☐ Nail polish (clear and any color you're wearing)
- ☐ Stain remover
- ☐ Safety pins
- ☐ Needle and thread
- ☐ Adhesive bandages
- ☐ Deodorant
- ☐ Tissues
- ☐ Lint roller
- ☐ Fashion tape
- ☐ Extra makeup (powder, lipstick, mascara)
- ☐ Bobby pins/hair ties
- ☐ Floss/mints
- ☐ Granola bar/portable snack
- ☐ Tampons
- ☐ Bottle of water

INFORMATION for GUESTS

As weddings become more destination oriented with guests often traveling, there are a number of things to consider that help limit questions and keep your sanity. From your website to the information section in your invitations, it's best to include travel and contact information in a number of places to cover all bases. Some guests are website savvy, while others are old-school and rely on the invitation to inform them. Finally, these recommendations are intended to allow your guests an easy, simple travel guide, and what you offer is completely up to you.

IMPORTANT INFORMATION

If you're opting for a wedding website, here's a checklist of essential information (and more!) to consider including.

☐ **Essentials**

    ☐ Names

    ☐ Wedding date

- [ ] Times (ceremony start)
- [ ] Ceremony location
- [ ] Reception location

- [ ] **Your story**

  - [ ] How you met
  - [ ] The proposal

- [ ] **Photos**

  - [ ] Engagement photos
  - [ ] Significant photos in your relationship
  - [ ] Photo of the outside of the venue, so that guests know what to expect

- [ ] **RSVP**

  - [ ] Instructions for how to RSVP
  - [ ] RSVP deadline

- [ ] **Schedule**

  - [ ] Pre-wedding events
  - [ ] Day-of schedule
  - [ ] Post-wedding events

- [ ] **The wedding party**

  - [ ] List the members of your wedding party, their relationship to you, and a cute photo of each

- [ ] **Travel information**
  - [ ] Closest airport
  - [ ] Hotel room block information
  - [ ] Local activities
  - [ ] Breakfast/lunch/dinner
  - [ ] Coffee shops
  - [ ] Bars or social activities
  - [ ] Outdoor activities
  - [ ] Shopping ideas
  - [ ] Cultural or historical experiences

- [ ] **Registry**
  - [ ] Provide a link to your various wedding registries

- [ ] **FAQs**
  - [ ] RSVP deadline
  - [ ] Dress code
  - [ ] Parking
  - [ ] Photos/social media sharing

- [ ] **Contact**
  - [ ] Create a wedding email address and direct all wedding-related questions there

HOTELS AND TRANSPORTATION

Because so many guests travel for weddings, including hotel recommendations and transportation options helps make their trip easy and limits the number of questions you field. The following are some quick tips.

Hotels

 Room blocks

- How many guests are traveling? _____

- Quick calculator: rooms for one-third of the total couples traveling (not total guest number) is recommended _____

- Price points: pick two at a lower/higher price point based on what your guests can afford _____

- Rooms must be booked before the deadline or they are released (one month pre-wedding)

☐ **Complimentary room block**

- Often fewer than 10 rooms per night

- Not guaranteed and is up to the hotel

- You're not financially responsible for any unbooked rooms

☐ **Contracted room block**

- 10 or more rooms per night for a small or boutique hotel

- You are contractually liable to fill or book a certain number of rooms, called "attrition"

- Better rates, but aim for a lower number of rooms so that you don't have to pay for any unbooked rooms

☐ **Discount codes**

- Ask larger hotel chains for discount codes as an alternative to room blocks. _____

TIP: If you reserve hotel blocks, it's better to underestimate and request more rooms to be added than to be stuck with the bill for any rooms that aren't booked.

Transportation

☐ **Between hotel and wedding venue**

    ☐ How many guests will need this? _____

    ☐ What kind of transportation is needed? (circle) 55-person bus/20- to 30-person passenger van/taxi/rideshare/other: _____

    ☐ Minimum amount of booked time per vehicle (often a 4-hour minimum, depending on the company) _____

☐ **Between hotel and after-party**

    ☐ How many guests will need this? _____

    ☐ What kind of transportation is needed? (circle) 55-person bus/20- to 30-person passenger van/taxi/rideshare/other: _____

REHEARSAL DINNER AND MORE

Events outside of the wedding itself have become more common, especially for destination weddings. Here is a list of other events to start brainstorming!

Pre- and Post-Wedding Activities

- [ ] Welcome dinner or drinks (common for destination weddings 2 nights prior to wedding)
- [ ] "Bridal" or group luncheon (optional, 1 or 2 days before wedding)
- [ ] Rehearsal dinner (night before wedding)
- [ ] Night-before nightcap (in lieu of a welcome or rehearsal dinner)
- [ ] After-party
- [ ] Day-after brunch

> **WEDDING WISDOM:** A bride had a complicated relationship with her mother, which made the wedding planning process tense at times. On the wedding day, her mom was anxious and stressed out. The bride had made an early decision to bring me in as an intermediary, and I recommended that there be a list of tasks for her mom to complete on the day, thus limiting her contact. Sometimes, the best way to ensure your happiness is to be honest about who you want around you on your wedding day and keep all those that bring more worry to you occupied with tasks and busy work.

REHEARSAL DINNER

Rehearsal dinners can be small and simple, or large and complex—whatever feels best for you and your guests. Here's a list with all the options to help you get started.

Rehearsal Dinner Tasks

☐ Determine guest list

    ☐ Traditional: bridal party and immediate family (#: _____)

    ☐ Destination wedding: any guest that is traveling (#: _____)

☐ Book the venue

☐ Choose the menu

☐ Decide on any decor: rentals, linens, candles, table assignments, menus _____

☐ Pick florist _____

☐ Decide on music: live music/DJ/playlist/none

☐ Send invitations: mail or digital

☐ Determine sound needs for music and toasts _____

☐ Determine who is giving toasts _____

☐ Give gifts to bridal party and VIPs (if giving)

CALL ANYONE BUT THE VIPS

Having the right team to field all the questions—including a missing officiant, a late bridal party, and venue directions—will help make your wedding day go smoothly.

- [ ] **Contact on the day of the wedding**

  - [ ] Make a "call list" for any questions

  - [ ] Call/text first: wedding planner or most responsible friend _____

  - [ ] Call/text second: maid of honor/ best man _____

  - [ ] Avoid putting the parents of the couple on this list, which can add extra stress to the day that you don't need!

  - [ ] Create a bridal party group chat for the wedding weekend (really helpful to answer all questions and keep everyone on time, and in the right locations).

  - [ ] Include your wedding planner or person in charge of making the day run smoothly

  - [ ] Avoid making yourself the main point of contact. Ask your most responsible friend or family member to do it, allowing you to be present and have fun!

  - [ ] Put enough information on the wedding website that people can easily refer to it for any issues.

HONEYMOON

Whether you've been daydreaming about the honeymoon or not, this is often the best part of wedding planning. Honeymoons can be short or long, you can opt to stick close by or travel across the globe, and you can jet off immediately after your wedding or wait until a better time—it's an opportunity for you two to spend some additional quality time together and relish your newlywed status. Here's how to keep the honeymoon planning as part of the agenda and get the creative juices going!

HONEYMOON TIMELINE

Use this checklist to brainstorm what kind of honeymoon you want to have, when and where you want to go, and how you're going to get there.

 Decide what kind of a trip you're taking and what you'd both like to do

- City/nature/beach/other: _____

☐ Longer honeymoon afar

- Over 1-week-long honeymoon

- Can include multiple destinations and activities

- Begin planning 10 months before wedding

- Place deposits 8 months before wedding for availability and pricing

☐ Mini-moon closer to home

- 2- to 7-night honeymoon

- Driving distance, or up to a 4- to 5-hour flight away

- Often single location

- Begin planning no less than 3 months before wedding for good rates and availability (except for holiday season)

> **TIP:** Honeymoon registries are in theory a great idea, but you tend to receive a lower-value gift through them than if your guests opt to give you a check to spend at your discretion. Instead, keep your registry short, and guests will often send a check instead of a formal gift, allowing you to put it towards your honeymoon and saving you the processing fee.

☐ Decide who is planning, how, and who is paying

_____

☐ Set a honeymoon budget _____
☐ Brainstorm activities or consult a travel agent

_____

_____

☐ Apply for your passport/confirm your passport is up-to-date
☐ Pack for honeymoon (at least 1 week in advance)
☐ Honeymoon registries

- Modern alternative to traditional registries
- Confirm processing percentage (often 2.5% of total) before committing
- Plan as though these are the cherry on top and not required for the trip
- Couples often receive less total cash through honeymoon registries than if guests were to give a cash gift

SECRET SPEND: If you're opting for a holiday-time honeymoon (which is from American Thanksgiving through the New Year), add an extra 2 months to the planning and be prepared for higher rates, especially in popular locales and accommodations.

APPENDIX I:
IMPORTANT NAMES AND NUMBERS

☐ Wedding planner/coordinator _____

☐ Ceremony venue _____

☐ Reception venue _____

☐ Photographer _____

☐ Videographer _____

☐ Caterer _____

☐ Cake/desserts _____

☐ Officiant _____

☐ Dress salon _____

☐ Hair _____

☐ Makeup _____

☐ Tailor _____

☐ Rentals _____

☐ Flowers _____

☐ Lighting _____

☐ Ceremony music _____

☐ Reception music _____

☐ Rehearsal dinner venue _____

☐ Transportation _____

☐ Stationery/paper goods _____

☐ VIP/best person: _____

- [ ] VIP/best person: _____
- [ ] VIP/alternate best person: _____

APPENDIX II: POST-WEDDING CHECKLIST

- [ ] Mail marriage license or coordinate with your officiant
- [ ] Return to venue to pick up left-behind items
- [ ] Return any rentals
- [ ] Record gifts or cards for thank-you notes
- [ ] Write thank-you notes (by three months post-wedding)
- [ ] If anyone changed their name, begin any documentation updates (social security, driver's license, etc.)
- [ ] Update financial information (joint bank accounts, financial beneficiaries, etc.)
- [ ] Create or update life insurance/wills
- [ ] Relax and enjoy married life!

APPENDIX III: NOTES

_____

_____

_____

_____

_____

About the Author

Elizabeth McKellar is the founder and creative director of the Nouveau Romantics, a nationally acclaimed wedding-planning and design company. With a background in architecture, Elizabeth began the Nouveau Romantics in 2010, honing her skills and expertise through hundreds of weddings across the United States and the world. Included on many lists of "Top Wedding Planner" by sources like *Harper's Bazaar*, *Martha Stewart Weddings*, and *Brides Magazine*, and published across the web on sites for *Style Me Pretty*, *Vogue*, and *Town and Country*, she's known for her seamless and cohesive design no matter the venue or locale. Though a native Canadian, she spends her time in Austin, Los Angeles, and her local airport hunting down the best tacos and ice cream, or else at home with her oversize black lab, Gus.

Connect with Elizabeth online:
Website: thenouveauromantics.com
Instagram: @thenouveauromantics
Facebook: facebook.com/thenouveauromantics